סדר ל ז״ יום השואה

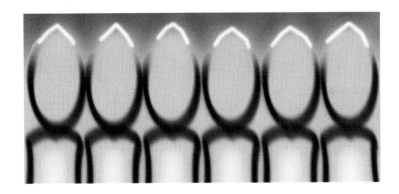

Haggadah
for the
Yom HaShoah Seder

Edited by Rabbi Avraham (Avi) Weiss

Coalition for Jewish Concerns—Amcha / Jonas Publishing

Printed in the United States of America by Atelier

ISBN: 0-615-11519-5

For additional copies of this book please call: 718 – 796 – 4730

Haggadah
for the
Yom HaShoah Seder

Acknowledgments

Over the past two years, in an effort to infuse lasting meaning to the historical reality of the Holocaust, we at the Hebrew Institute of Riverdale have conducted a Yom HaShoah Seder on Holocaust Remembrance Day. We have found this Seder to be invaluable in helping to shape a ritual observance that could prevent the Shoah from being lost to memory. This Haggadah was born of that initiative and, like the Passover Haggadah, has evolved into the text that guides us as we seek each year to evoke the Shoah with fresh and piercing immediacy. Our experience with the Seder and the Haggadah that grew out of it has inspired us to reach out to the Jewish community at large in order to share what we have learned.

The Haggadah for the Yom HaShoah Seder brings together the ideas, creativity and commitment of many individuals who have played vital roles in its development. Rabbi Aaron Frank, Associate Rabbi at HIR, and Rabbi Barry Gelman, former Associate Rabbi at HIR and now Rabbi of Congregation Shaar Hashomayim in Montreal, made extraordinary contributions to the conceptualization, formulation, and compilation of the Haggadah. Rabbi Yosef Kanefsky, another former Associate Rabbi at HIR and now Rabbi of Congregation B'nai David in Los Angeles, was there at the beginning, helping to bring the project to life.

Jeffrey S. Gurock, Libby M. Klaperman Professor of American Jewish History at Yeshiva University, who composed the original text of the readings, attorney Laura Shaw Frank, who recorded the testimony of the survivors, and Michael Horen, Director of Special Projects at IDT, who designed and produced the entire project, brought their formidable intelligence and gifts as well as their unique knowledge and skills, to the shaping of the content and presentation of the Haggadah. We are deeply grateful to them.

Credit should be given to YIVO for making available some of the dramatic readings and Yiddish songs. Special recognition and thanks are also due to Illene Burack for her generous support.

The publication of the Haggadah would not have been possible without the support of Debbie and Howard Jonas. We are immensely indebted to them for their generosity. They have given concrete expression to both their profound understanding of the imperative of zachor and their keen appreciation of the need for a formalized ritual practice to carry out that imperative. May they and all those who have contributed to this Haggadah be forever blessed for "remembering."

Rabbi Avi Weiss,
New York,
Adar II, 5760
April, 2000

We suggest that this Haggadah be read in a darkened room. Participants may be seated in a circle. Those who are able should sit on the floor. Yahrzeit candles are placed in the center. Six large candles representing the six million should be set up and lit at the designated time.

Opening Thoughts—*narrator reads:*

Just as the Haggadah provides an eternal framework for each of us to experience the Exodus from Egypt, so, too, a ritual for remembering the Holocaust—the greatest catastrophe that ever befell the Jewish people—is needed to transform Yom HaShoah from a day in which we are spectators to one in which we feel like participants.

Until now, we have relied on the survivors of the Holocaust, the eyewitnesses, to tell their stories. On Yom HaShoah—Holocaust Remembrance Day—we listen to the testimony of the survivors with even greater attention and reverence in order to absorb what they have endured in every fiber of our being.

But soon the only ones left to tell the story will be those who did not live through the events themselves. It will fall to succeeding generations, as the Passover Haggadah teaches, to repeat the narrative and re-experience it as if they themselves were there.

Thus, we must now begin to transfer the task of zachor—of remembrance—to the next generation. The Shoah will be remembered only if all Jews can declare, "Although we were not physically there, we too are survivors."

What follows is an attempt to create such an observance. There is no event in Jewish history that is remembered without ritual. Only through a formalized ritual, enacted each year on Yom HaShoah, as the Exodus from Egypt is enacted each year on Passover, can we prevent the Holocaust from becoming a footnote in Jewish history.

Introduction — *narrator reads:*

Tonight, through this Yom HaShoah Seder, we enact a ritual in the form of a Seder for the remembrance of the Shoah.

This Seder consists of four parts:

Churban Gashmi (Physical Destruction)	חורבן גשמי
Churban Ruchani (Spiritual Destruction)	חורבן רוחני
Churban Banim U'Vanot	חורבן בנים
(Destruction of Children)	ובנות
Gevurah (Resistance)	גבורה

Each part, in turn, will effect memory
through four activities:

Hachanah (Preparatory Focus)	הכנה
Dibbur (Verbalization)	דבור
Reading in Unison	
Testimony	
Song	
Reading	
Ma'aseh (Re-enactment)	מעשה
Machshavah (Reflection)	מחשבה

Through the ritual enactment of each of the four parts of this Seder, we shall strive to feel as if we ourselves were there, as if we too are survivors, as if we too experienced the Shoah.

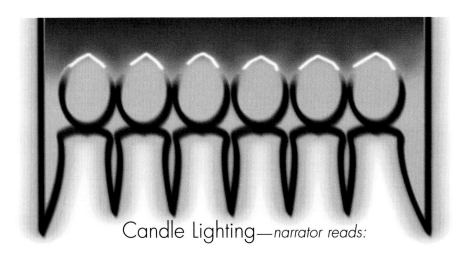

Candle Lighting—*narrator reads:*

We begin by inviting survivors of the Shoah to come forward to light six candles as we sing Ani Ma'amin, the Jewish anthem of ultimate faith sung by many during the Holocaust. Please rise. (The narrator calls out the names of survivors chosen to light the candles. One by one they come forward.)

אֲנִי מַאֲמִין בֶּאֱמוּנָה שְׁלֵמָה,
בְּבִיאַת הַמָּשִׁיחַ אֲנִי מַאֲמִין,
וְאַף עַל פִּי שֶׁיִּתְמַהְמֵהַּ,
עִם כָּל זֶה אֲנִי מַאֲמִין.

Ani ma'amin, be'emunah shelema,
b'viat HaMashiach, ani ma'amin,
v'af al pi she'yitmameha
im kol ze, ani ma'amin.

I believe with perfect faith
in the coming of the Messiah,
I believe.
And though He tarry, I believe.

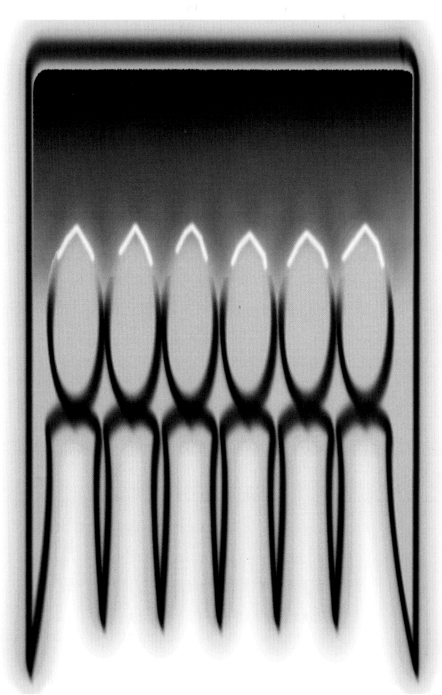

(After lighting the candles, a siren is sounded for one minute simulating the moment of rememberence as observed in Israel on Yom HaShoah.)

PART I:
CHURBAN GASHMI—PHYSICAL DESTRUCTION

1. Hachanah—Preparatory Focus—*narrator reads:*

The Shoah brought about the near decimation of the Jewish population of Europe. Six million Jewish souls were extinguished in a devastating physical destruction, a Churban Gashmi. Let us pause now and focus our thoughts before we speak of what occurred.

2. Dibbur—Verbalization—*reading in unison:*

As Jews entered the modern world, they wanted to believe that a nearly two-thousand-year-old legacy of religious hatred had ended. The rise of modern anti-Semitism in the late nineteenth century did not deter the Jewish drive for complete and sustained emancipation. After World War I, German Jewry looked optimistically toward a future of increased acceptance and economic advancement in their homeland

But the evil one, who rose to power in 1933 along with his henchmen, masterfully wove together the medieval anti-Semitism of the church and new theories of racial superiority, which swept along millions of Germans who were open to accept his message or too complacent to oppose it. Jews were considered untermenschen, lower forms of life, to be eliminated from the universe.

Kristallnacht, in November 1938, was an ominous foreboding of what was to come. A long, violent night of rampage and destruction left the ancient synagogues of Germany and Austria shattered and vast numbers of Jewish properties destroyed.

The systematic elimination of the Jews began in September 1939, with the start of World War II. The "Final Solution of the Jewish People" proceeded in three stages, mounting in intensity in the wake of German conquests. First, ghettos were established. Then, in 1941, with the invasion of Russia, Einsatzgruppen, mobile killing units, began operations. Finally, the annihilation of millions of Jews from every European country—west to east, religious and secular, Ashkenazim and Sephardim, was carried out by gassing, by slave labor, or by atrocious perverted medical experimentation in the death camps. As the atrocities unfolded, nations and individuals stood by in silence. The Vatican, too, turned its back on the Jews of Europe.

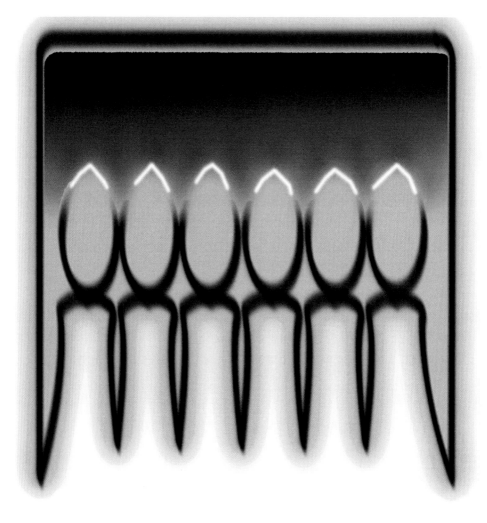

Testimony: A survivor comes forward to give a personal account of Churban Gashmi—PhysicalDestruction. (If no survivor is present to offer this testimony, someone may be designated to read this account as given by Bernard Adler.)

The Nazis rounded us up to leave our village. Every family got a wagon. We left all our belongings in the house. We had a cat, and we left the cat behind. We got close to the city. My father had a very long beard. He was a Satmarer Chassid. An SS went up and jumped on the wagon, and took a match to my father's beard. My father was starting to scream. My mother was crying. My two sisters were on the wagon, and my mother and my father. He was still alive after they burned his beard. Then they shaved him. They shaved all the men in the ghetto.

On the second day of Shavuos, the Nazis told us we were leaving the ghetto. They took us to the railroad and put us in a train car with no seats. They put fifty or sixty people in each car with a dish for a toilet. The train stopped when we came into Krakow. There was a drop window in the train car. It was closed, and sealed shut with wire. My youngest sister was two years younger than I was. I was the eighth child and she was the ninth in my family. I loved her so much. She was my life. The older children were off doing their own things, but my younger sister and I—we were so close to each other. I loved her so much. She heard the SS talking outside and she went to look outside that drop window. All of the sudden I heard a shot. They shot her in the head. She fell into my hands. We were starting to scream, so an SS opened a door and he said, "One thing I can tell you is that if you make any noise I will shoot the whole car and the whole car will be dead." We quieted down, What could we do? We were with her almost two days, dead, until we got to Auschwitz.

Song: Al Eleh Ani Bochiya (Lamentations 1:16)—*all join in*

עַל אֵלֶּה אֲנִי בוֹכִיָּה
עֵינִי עֵינִי יֹרְדָה מַּיִם
כִּי רָחַק מִמֶּנִּי
מְנַחֵם מֵשִׁיב
נַפְשִׁי

Al eleh ani bochiya,
Eyni eyni yorda mayim
Ki rachak mimeni
menachem meysheev
nafshi

For these I weep,
My eye runs with water
For the comforter who
would have restored my soul
is far from me

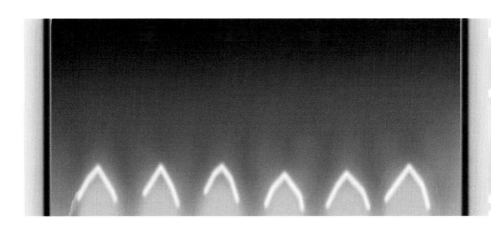

Reading: Es Brent—*all join in*
(words and music by Mordechai Gebirtig)

ס׳ברענט! בר׳דערלעך, ס׳ברענט!
אוי, אונדזער אָרעם שטעטל נעבעך ברענט!
בײַזע ווינטן מיט ירגזון
רײַסן, ברעכן און צעבלאָזן
שטאַרקער נאָך די ווילדע פלאַמען,
אַלץ אַרום שוין ברענט.
און איר שטייט און קוקט אַזוי זיך
מיט פאַרלייגטע הענט,
און איר שטייט און קוקט אַזוי זיך –
אונדזער שטעטל ברענט!

Es brent, bri-der-lech, es brent
Oi un-zer o-rem shte-tl ne-bech brent
Be'-ze vin-tn mit yir-go-zun
Rai-sn bre-chn un tsu-bloi-zn
Shtar-ker noch di vil-de flam-en
Alts a-rum shoin brent
Un ir shte't un kukt a-zoi zich
Mit far-le'g-te hent
Un ir shte't un kukt a-zoi zich
Un-zer shte-tl brent!

It is burning, dear brothers, it is burning!
Our poor little town is burning!
Angry winds whip the flames.
Everything is on fire!
And you stand helplessly
With folded hands and stare
While the flames grow higher
And our little town burns.

3. Ma'aseh—Re-enactment—*narrator reads:*

In this Churban Gashmi, this mass physical destruction, not only were lives and property destroyed, but personal dignity was also extinguished. We now ask you to remove your shoes and place them behind you. To symbolically experience the loss of all our possessions, we ask you to remove your watch and jewelry, and to empty your pockets; please place all items in the box in front of you.

4. Machshavah—Reflection—*narrator reads:*

Having re-enacted the Churban Gashmi, we pause now to reflect on how each of us would have encountered such horrors. First we were shorn of our possessions. Then we were shorn of our dignity. Then we were shorn of our lives. We imagine ourselves as if we had personally, each one of us, experienced the Shoah.

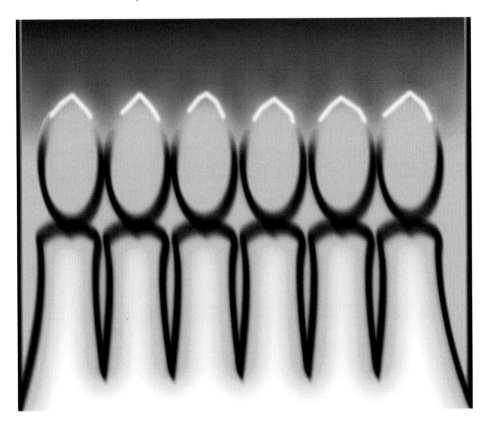

PART II:
CHURBAN RUCHANI—SPIRITUAL DESTRUCTION

1. Hachanah—Preparatory Focus—*narrator reads:*

Not only were six million Jews physically murdered, but the evil one also sought to destroy our religious and spiritual life—to bring about a Churban Ruchani, a Spiritual Destruction. Let us pause now and focus our thoughts before we speak of what occurred.

2. Dibbur—Verbalization—*reading in unison:*

A world of souls was destroyed by the evil one, and, at the same time, the soul of a people was imperiled. A millennium of religious and cultural creativity was extinguished as the victims perished. In an effort to calculate the enormity of the tragedy, Professor Salo Baron told the Eichmann trial: "It is no exaggeration to say that Polish Jewry alone produced between 1937 and 1939 more works of Torah than in any decade of the seventeenth or eighteenth century."

These scholars were heirs to a five-hundred-year-old tradition of yeshiva learning that was the glory of Poland and the pride of Lithuania. They produced a body of literature that enriched not only enthusiastic lamdanim, or educators, and ba'ale batim, or householders, in Eastern Europe, but also Jews in America, Zion, and elsewhere in the world. Eastern European Jewry could have continued a flowering of rabbinic learning for another thousand years. That world was destroyed.

Among secular Jews, too, the period before 1939 included years of great intellectual and artistic creativity. Scores of journals, periodicals, and books in Hebrew, Yiddish, Ladino, as well as the local languages were produced by Jews on Jewish and general topics. These writers and thinkers are no more.

What did the world lose because Jewish blood was so cheap? Eminent Jewish scientists and scholars in medicine, law, and numerous other fields who brought honor and renown to their native countries were put to death merely because they were Jews. When we mourn a Jewish world that was lost, we must also mourn the loss to the world of what these victims, so cruelly annihilated, could have contributed.

Testimony: A survivor comes forward to give a personal account of Churban Ruchani—Spiritual Destruction. (If no survivor is present to offer this testimony, someone may be designated to read this account as given by Carola Greenspan.)

Near the end of the war, we were sent to the death camp Stutthof. The Germans were in a hurry to kill us all not only physically, but spiritually. Only a handful of people survived Stutthof. As long as I was in the ghetto and I had my one skirt and blouse and the hair on my head, I was a person. When I was taken to the camps I lost all of that. We had to call each other's names because we were unrecognizable. We had lost our sense of being unique, of being created in the image of God. We slept on a dirt floor and had nothing to eat. We were starving—starving not only for physical food, but also for spiritual food. Our Jewish books had been stripped from us.

One day, a German came from the labor bureau because he needed someone to pick potatoes. He picked me and two other girls. We were overjoyed because we thought that maybe we would get some food there. But when we got there, we found that we had to pick the potatoes with our bare hands. A cold rain was falling. Every day, I put on the same clothing, and it was like a sheet of ice from that rain. After some time, I was injured falling off a wagon and I could not work anymore, so they took me back to Stuthoff on a train. I saw civilians reading newspapers on the train, but they refused to look at me.

I was nothing. My soul didn't count. I weighed about 80 pounds then. They buried their faces in the paper. The Germans made me ride back to Stuthoff between two freight cars of the train in the freezing cold. There is no answer to how I survived. Faith got me through.

Song: Shomer Yisrael—all join in

שׁוֹמֵר יִשְׂרָאֵל,
שְׁמֹר שְׁאֵרִית יִשְׂרָאֵל,
וְאַל יֹאבַד יִשְׂרָאֵל,
הָאֹמְרִים, שְׁמַע יִשְׂרָאֵל.

(from the morning prayer service)
Shomer Yisrael,
Shemor sh'airit Yisrael,
Ve'al yovad Yisrael,
Ha'omrim Shema Yisrael

O Guardian of Israel,
protect the remnant of Israel;
let not Israel be destroyed,
those who proclaim, "Hear O Israel."

Reading:
A Prayer Before Eating Hametz—*all join in*
(Bergen Belsen, 1944; there were no matzot in Bergen Belsen for Passover 1944. It was decided that bread could be eaten preceded by this prayer.)

Our Father in Heaven: You surely know that it is our desire to do Your will, and to observe Pesach by eating matza and by observing the prohibition concerning hametz. But to our great distress, our situation prevents us from doing so, and our lives are hanging in the balance. As such, we are hereby prepared and ready to fulfill the mitzvah of "living by Torah, and not dying by it." And so our prayer before You is that You allow us to live on, and that You redeem us, so that we can soon fulfill Your laws and serve You with a fuller heart. Amen.

3. Ma'aseh—Re-enactment—*narrator reads:*

In this Churban Ruchani, this Spiritual Destruction, Jewish learning was under attack. To re-enact the pain of the loss of opportunities for learning, we take a sheet imprinted with the Hebrew alphabet, the alef-bet, symbolic of our Torah, and rip it in half. We place the torn pages in the center of our circle and set them on fire. As in the story of the Ten Martyrs, the parchment burns, but the letters ascend toward heaven. (Each participant should now rip up the copy they have before them of the aleph-bet sheet that appears at the end of this Haggadah.)

4. Machshavah—Reflection—*narrator reads:*

Having re-enacted the Churban Ruchani, we pause now to reflect on how each of us would have encountered such horrors. First we were shorn of our possessions. Then we were shorn of our dignity. Then we were shorn of our lives. We imagine ourselves as if we had personally, each one of us, experienced the Shoah.

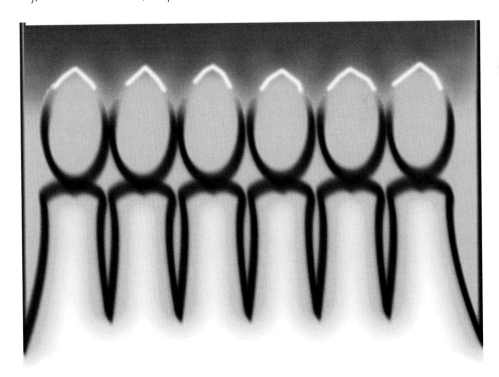

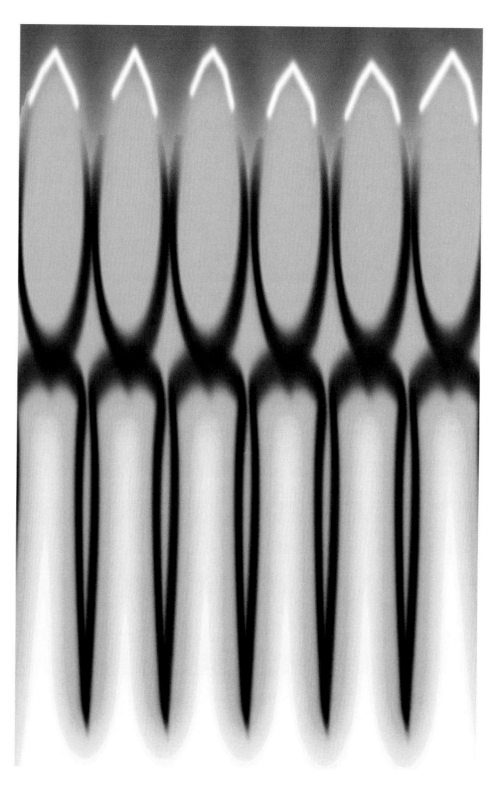

PART III: CHURBAN BANIM U'VANOT— DESTRUCTION OF CHILDREN

1. Hachanah—Preparatory Focus—*narrator reads:*

The Churban Banim U'Vanot brought about the breakup of countless families and the murder of one million of our children—our link to the future, the symbol of our hopes and dreams. Let us pause now and focus our thoughts before we speak of what occurred.

2. Dibbur—Verbalization—*reading in unison:*

From the abyss, the Chasidic Rebbe, Kalonimus Kalmish Shapiro, cried out, "How can the universe remain standing and not turn into chaos?"

How do we fathom the deaths of almost a million and a half children? Today they would have been among our teachers and leaders, writers and poets, rabbis and artists. They would have been the mothers and fathers of a Jewish world that is no more.

In 1930, for example, nearly one hundred and twenty thousand Jews lived in Bohemia, Moravia, and Silesia. By October 1945, only fourteen thousand remained, among them only twelve hundred children. At Auschwitz-Birkenau, it was the children and their mothers, the weakest and least useful for slave labor, who were selected first for extermination.

Why were they murdered? The answer, on one level, can be found in the irrationality of the evil one's anti-Semitism. All Jews were equal in their eyes; all Jews were enemies. The youngest child and the sage were all linked together by the evil one's hatred. But even more terrible was the evil one's recognition that children were, as they have always been, the future. We will never know what those murdered children would have contributed to our communities, to our people and to the world. We can only hold fast to our own children, our own future generation. We can only strive to safeguard the continuity of our people.

Testimony: A survivor comes forward to give a personal account of Churban Banim U'Vanot—Destruction of Children (If no survivor is present to offer this testimony, someone may be designated to read this account as given by Dora Prawer.)

During the war, I was living with my aunt. She was ill with breast cancer and she had no children, so I, a young teenager, stayed with her to care for her. My parents and my two sisters lived in another ghetto. I knew I had try to go see them because I had a feeling it would be the last time I would see them. I couldn't take a train because then they would know I was a Jew. I had no false papers. So, I took off my Jewish star and took a chance. I went to stand on the highway to search for a ride. I was fifteen, but made myself look younger. The road was full of German soldiers. Some soldiers stopped, and I went with them. I spoke perfect German, so they didn't know who I really was. I was so frightened that they would find out who I was and shoot me. I tried to make my cheeks look red so I would look healthy. I got to my parents' ghetto, and I got to see my parents, but my sisters were not there. I never got to see them again because after I left, all the Jews in their ghetto were gathered together and shot.

When they liquidated the ghetto that my aunt and I lived in, we were all called to the marketplace. They told us they were going to give us new identification cards. I, being so young, was holding onto my aunt so hard so they wouldn't separate us. A German soldier had to kick me to separate me from her. He kicked me so hard that I went flying through the air and hit my head. I had seizures after that. That was the last time I saw my aunt.

Song: Oyfn Pripenchik—*all join in*
(words and music by M. Warshawsky)

אויפֿן פּריפּעטשיק ברענט אַ פֿייערל,

און אין שטוב איז הייס.

און דער רבי לערנט קלײַנע קינדערלעך

דעם אַלף־בית.

רעפֿרײן:

זעט זשע, קינדערלעך, געדענקט זשע, טײַערע,

וואָס איר לערנט דאָ,

זאָגט זשע נאָך אַ מאָל

און טאַקע נאָך אַ מאָל:

קמץ־אַלף: אָ!

לערנט, קינדער, מיט גרויס חשק,

אַזוי זאָג איך אײַך אָן,

ווער ס'וועט ביכער פֿון אײַך קענען עבֿרי,

דער באַקומט אַ פֿאָן.

אַז איר וועט, קינדער, עלטער ווערן,

וועט איר אַלײן פֿאַרשטײן,

וויפֿל אין די אותיות ליגן טרערן,

און ווי פֿיל געוויין.

אַז איר וועט, קינדער, דעם גלות שלעפֿן,

אויסגעמוטשעט זײַן,

זאָלט איר פֿון די אותיות

כוח שעפֿן,

קוקט אין זיי אַרײַן!

Oyfn pripenchik brent a fay-erl,
Un in shtub iz heys.
Un der rebbe lernt kleyne kinderlach
Dem alef-beyz.

Refrain:
Zet zha, kinderlekh, gedenkt zha, tayera,
Vos ir lernt do,
Zogt zhe noch a mol:
Un taka noch a mol
Komets aleph oh.

Lernt, kinder, mit groys cheyshek,
Azoy zog ich eich on,
Ver s'vet bicher fun eich kenen ivre,
Der bakumt a fon.

Az ir vet, kinder, alter vern,
Vet ir aleyn farshtayn,
Vifil in di oysyes lign trern,
Un vi fil geveyn.

Az ir vet, kinder, dem goles shlepn,
Oysgemutshet zayn
Zolt ir fun di oysyes
Koyech shepn
Kukt in zey arayn!

A flame burns in the fireplace,
the room warms up,
as the teacher drills the children
in the alef-bet.

Refrain:
Remember dear children,
what you are learning here.
Repeat it again
and again:
komets-alef is pronounced oh.

Dear children,
learn with great enthusiasm.
Whoever learns to read well
will receive a reward.

When you grow older
you will understand
that this alphabet contains
the tears and the weeping of our people.

When you grow weary
and burdened with exile,
you will find
comfort and strength
within this Jewish alphabet.

Reading: I Never Saw Another Butterfly —*all join in*
(4.6.1942, Pavel Friedmann)

The last, the very last,
So richly, brightly, dazzlingly yellow.
Perhaps if the sun's tears would sing
against a white stone...

Such, such a yellow
Is carried lightly 'way up high.
It went away I'm sure because it wished to
kiss the world good-bye.

For seven weeks I've lived in here,
Penned up inside this ghetto.
But I have found what I love here.
The dandelions call to me
And the white chestnut branches in the court.
Only I never saw another butterfly.

That butterfly was the last one.
Butterflies don't live in here,
in the ghetto.

3. Ma'aseh—Re-enactment—*narrator reads:*

In the Churban Banim U'Vanot, as we seek to experience the suffering of families torn apart, we ask all children to separate from their parents and move to the special section in the corner.

(Children move to a roped off area in a corner of the room.)

4. Machshavah—Reflection—*narrator reads:*

Having re-enacted the Churban Banim U'Vanot, we pause now to reflect on how each of us would have encountered such horrors. First we were shorn of our possessions. Then we were shorn of our dignity. Then we were shorn of our lives. We imagine ourselves as if we had personally, each one of us, experienced the Shoah.

PART IV: GEVURAH—RESISTANCE

1. Hachanah—Preparatory Focus—*narrator reads:*
Tonight is not only Yom HaShoah, a day to remember the destruction; it is also Yom HaShoah Ve'ha'Gevurah, a day to remember the inspiring physical and spiritual heroism of our people as they resisted the assaults of the evil one. Let us pause now and focus our thoughts before we speak of what occurred.

2. Dibbur—Verbalization—*reading in unison:*
In the midst of the darkness of the Holocaust, we desperately seek the light of heroism. We search for the names of the heroes who led the uprising in Treblinka and the courageous fighters of the Warsaw Ghetto. We take pride in the exploits of the Jewish partisan fighters who took up arms against all odds and, alone and abandoned, fought the enemy.

But the light of heroism encompasses the vast majority of Jews, including those who perished, those who manifested spiritual resistance. We recall the unnamed teachers who continued teaching in the ghetto schools, thereby declaring to the world that even in the face of death, the learning of Torah must go on. We recall the many whose identity as Jews was strengthened in the ghettos, among them those who could have passed on the Aryan side but chose instead to share the fate of their people. We recall the courageous editors and writers who published clandestine newspapers to raise the spirit of their fellow Jews. All of these journals and written accounts from the ghettos and the camps were inspired by a single overriding, urgent imperative: to make sure the world will know what had happened.

We recall, finally, the heroism of the survivor generation, the sheayrit ha'pelaytah, who, despite the devastating losses they suffered, moved beyond despair to rebuild their lives, enriching all of us materially and spiritually over the years.

All those who were victims of the Shoah are holy. Tonight we seek to partake in some measure of their holiness by attempting to relive their experience. Those who went to their death with Shema Yisrael on their lips are holy believers and those who went to their death asking "Where is God?" are no less holy. They are, in Rabbi Eliezer Berkovits' words, "holy disbelievers."

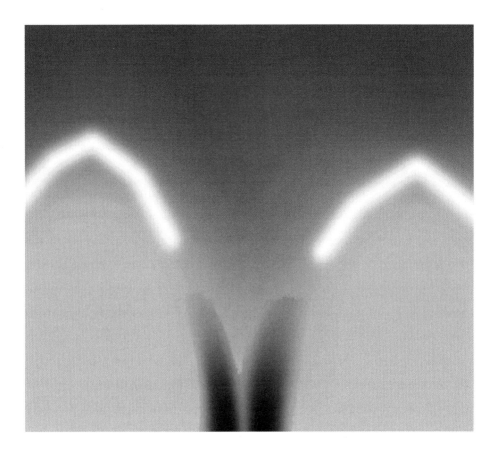

Testimony: A survivor comes forward now to give a personal account of Gevurah—Resistance.

(If no survivor is present to offer this testimony, someone may be designated to read this account as given by Helen Balsam.)

My husband when he was a young man in the camps overheard a German commandant telling another German how much he needed gasoline for his motorcycle. This German was a killer. If he could kill a Jew – he wouldn't give a hoot. My husband wanted to do something to get on the good side of him. He was working outside with Polish political prisoners who were not as incarcerated as we were. They could get certain things. So my husband asked them to get him some gasoline, and they did. The next day he brought the German a bottle of gasoline in his pants. At first the German started yelling and screaming, "How dare you? Are you trying to bribe me?" But he accepted it, because he needed that gasoline, and he gave my husband bread. Almost every day my husband brought the German some gasoline and because of this, my husband could get bread. He had a plan of how to survive.

When we were liberated by the American army, they were afraid to come into the camps because there was TB and dystentery – all sorts of infectious diseases. Most of us were taken to hospitals, and many people died in the hospitals. I was very sick, but I was getting better. It was Spring – May, June, and it was a beautiful world out there. We were very weak, but we wanted to live. We wanted to enjoy this beautiful world. We did our best to get better. We tried to be happy. We were very young still, and wanted to enjoy life. In the Displaced Person Camp where I was, the girls were pairing up with the guys. There is something in us that wanted to go on. It's a God-given instinct.

Reading: The Dry Bones—*all join in*
(Auschwitz, 1959, by Rabbi Dr. Moshe Weiss)

There I stood on a little hill
In the Auschwitz Death Camp
Surrounded by blocks and barracks
Where inmates lived, suffered, died
Under the black smokestacks of the ovens,
Encircled by the stark whiteness of snow and ash and bone.
The Polish guide explained,
"The grass on these plains
grows abundantly in summer and spring,
blue grass fed by the fertilizer under the soil.
Come back after winter and see how lovely it is!"

There I stood, praying the ashes could somehow cohere,
Recalling the question posed to Ezekiel in the valley,
"Can these bones live?"
And there came a noise, a shaking, and the bones
Came together, bone to his bone,
The sinews and the flesh upon them,
And the skin covered them above,
And the breath came into them and they lived,
And stood up upon their feet, an exceeding great army.
"Behold O my people,
I will open your graves,
And cause you to come out of your graves,
And bring you to the land of Israel."

There I stood, on a lofty mountain
In Jerusalem.
Before me, the vast host of the Jewish people.
In schoolrooms, in cities, in factories, in villages,
In battle, in peace.
God, remember the souls of the departed
And guard over the resurrected children of Israel
In the land of Israel.

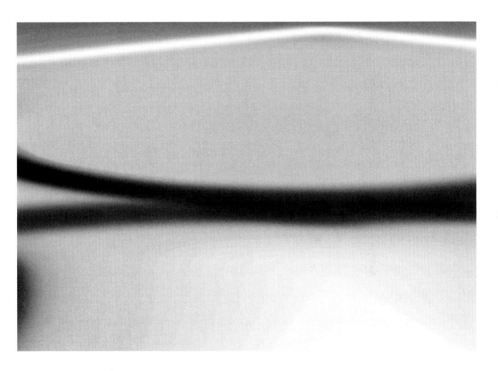

3. Ma'aseh—Re-enactment—*narrator reads:*

As Gevurah led to a reclaiming of personal dignity, we now ask you to put your shoes back on, to replace your watches and jewelry and the contents of your pockets; we ask children to rejoin their parents; and we ask everyone to stand as we sing Shir HaPartizanim, the Partisan's Hymn. We give honor to all who resisted, physically and spiritually—those who perished and those who survived.

Song: Shir HaPartizanim—Partisan's Hymn

Survivors are called forward to lead this song as all join in
(words by Hirsh Glick, music by Dmitri Pokrass)

זאָג ניט קיין מאָל, אַז דו גייסט דעם לעצטן וועג.
כאָטש הימלען בלײַענע פאַרשטעלן בלויע טעג.
קומען וועט נאָך אונדזער אויסגעבענקטע שעה,
עס וועט אַ פויק טאָן אונדזער טראָט – מיר זײַנען דאָ!

פון גרינעם פאַלמענלאַנד ביז ווײַסן לאַנד פון שניי,
מיר קומען אָן מיט אונדזער פּײַן, מיט אונדזער וויי,
און וווּ געפאַלן ס'איז אַ שפּריץ פון אונדזער בלוט,
שפּראָצן וועט דאָרט אונדזער גבורה, אונדזער מוט.

עס וועט די מאָרגנזון באַגילדן אונדז דעם הײַנט.
און דער נעכטן וועט פאַרשווינדן מיטן פײַנד.
נאָר אויב פאַרזאַמען וועט די זון אין דעם קאַיאָר –
ווי אַ פּאַראָל זאָל גיין דאָס ליד פון דור צו דור.

דאָס ליד געשריבן איז מיט בלוט און ניט מיט בלײַ,
ס'איז ניט קיין לידל פון אַ פויגל אויף דער פרײַ,
דאָס האָט אַ פאָלק צווישן פאַלנדיקע ווענט
דאָס ליד געזונגען מיט נאַגאַנעס אין די הענט.

טאָ זאָג ניט קיין מאָל, אַז דו גייסט דעם לעצטן וועג,
כאָטש הימלען בלײַענע פאַרשטעלן בלויע טעג.
קומען וועט נאָך אונדזער אויסגעבענקטע שעה –
עס וועט אַ פויק טאָן אונדזער טראָט – מיר זײַנען דאָ!

Never say this is the final road for you,
Though leaden skies may cover over days of blue.
As the hour that we longed for is so near,
Our step beats out the message—we are here!

From lands so green with palms to lands all white with snow,
We shall be coming with our anguish and our woe,
And where a spurt of our blood fell on the earth,
There our courage and our spirit have rebirth.

The early morning sun will brighten our day,
And yesterday with our foe will fade away.
But if the sun delays and in the east remains—
This song as password generations must maintain.

This song was written with our blood and not with lead,
It's not a little tune that birds sing overhead.
This song a people sang amid collapsing walls,
With grenades in hands they heeded to the call.

Therefore never say the road now ends for you.
Though leaden skies may cover over days of blue.
As the hour that we longed for is so near
Our step beats out the message—we are here!

4. Machshavah—Reflection—*narrator reads:*
Having re-enacted Gevurah, we pause now to reflect on how each of us would have encountered such horrors. First we were shorn of our possessions. Then we were shorn of our dignity. Then we were shorn of our lives. We imagine ourselves as if we had personally, each one of us, experienced the Shoah.

The Food of the Camps—*narrator reads:*
We now pass around potato peels. As we eat this poor food we try to feel even more sharply the pain of our sisters and brothers during the Shoah

Final Prayers and Hatikva—*narrator reads:*
We have reflected, retold, and re-experienced. We conclude with Kel Maleh Rachamim and Kaddish, the prayers for the dead, followed by Hatikva, Israel's national anthem. When you return home, please remember to light a yahrzeit candle in memory of the six million. Please rise

אֵל מָלֵא רַחֲמִים שׁוֹכֵן בַּמְּרוֹמִים.

הַמְצֵא מְנוּחָה נְכוֹנָה עַל כַּנְפֵי הַשְּׁכִינָה.

בְּמַעֲלוֹת קְדוֹשִׁים וּטְהוֹרִים

כְּזֹהַר הָרָקִיעַ מַזְהִירִים

אֶת נִשְׁמוֹת הַקְּדוֹשִׁים וְהַטְּהוֹרִים

שֶׁהֻשְׁמְדוּ וְשֶׁנֶּהֶרְגוּ וְשֶׁנִּשְׁחֲטוּ וְשֶׁנִּשְׂרְפוּ

וְשֶׁנִּטְבְּעוּ וְשֶׁנֶּחְנְקוּ

עַל קִידוּשׁ הַשֵׁם

בַּעֲבוּר שֶׁאֶתֵּן צְדָקָה בְּעַד הַזְכָּרַת נִשְׁמָתֵיהֶם,

בְּגַן עֵדֶן תְּהֵא מְנוּחָתָם.

לָכֵן בַּעַל הָרַחֲמִים

יַסְתִּירֵם בְּסֵתֶר כְּנָפָיו לְעוֹלָמִים.

וְיִצְרוֹר בִּצְרוֹר הַחַיִּים אֶת נִשְׁמָתָם,

יְיָ הוּא נַחֲלָתָם:

וְיָנוּחוּ בְּשָׁלוֹם עַל מִשְׁכְּבוֹתֵהֶם. וְנֹאמַר אָמֵן:

AYL MALEH RACHAMIM

Ayl maleh rachamim Shochayn bam'romim,

Ham-tzay m'nucha n'chona al kanfay Hash'china

B'ma-alot k'doshim ut-horim

K'zo-har horoki-a mazhirim,

Et nishmot hak'doshim v'hat'horim

She'hushmedu v'shenehergu v'shenishchatu v'shenis-r'fu

v'shenit-b'u v'shenechneku

al kidush Ha-Shaym

Ba'avur she'etayn tz'dakah b'ad hazkorat nishmatam.

B'Gan Ayden t'hay m'nuchatam,

La-chayn Ba-al Horachamim

Yas-tiraym b'sayter k'nofov le'olomim,

V'yitz-ror bitz-ror hacha-yim et nishomotam,

Adonoy hu na-chalatam,

V'yonuchu b'sholom al mishk'votay-hem

V'nomar: Amen.

FOR MARTYRS

O God full of mercy, who dwells on high, grant proper rest on the wings of the Divine Presence in the lofty levels of the holy and the pure ones who shine like the glow of the firmament, for the souls of the holy and pure ones who were killed, murdered, slaughtered, burned, drowned, and strangled for the sanctification of the Name. Because I shall give to charity in remembrance of their souls. May their resting place be in the Garden of Eden. Therefore may the Master of Mercy shelter them in the shelter of His wings for eternity: And may He bind their souls in the bond of life. Hashem is their heritage, and may they repose in peace on their resting places. Now let us respond: Amen.

MOURNER'S KADDISH—*all join in*

יִתְגַּדַּל וְיִתְקַדַּשׁ שְׁמֵהּ רַבָּא.
(אָמֵן)
בְּעָלְמָא דִּי בְרָא כִרְעוּתֵהּ.
וְיַמְלִיךְ מַלְכוּתֵהּ,
בְּחַיֵּיכוֹן וּבְיוֹמֵיכוֹן
וּבְחַיֵּי דְכָל בֵּית יִשְׂרָאֵל,
בַּעֲגָלָא וּבִזְמַן קָרִיב.
וְאִמְרוּ: אָמֵן.
(אָמֵן.
יְהֵא שְׁמֵהּ רַבָּא מְבָרַךְ לְעָלַם וּלְעָלְמֵי עָלְמַיָּא).
יִתְבָּרַךְ וְיִשְׁתַּבַּח וְיִתְפָּאַר
וְיִתְרוֹמַם וְיִתְנַשֵּׂא
וְיִתְהַדָּר וְיִתְעַלֶּה וְיִתְהַלָּל
שְׁמֵהּ דְּקֻדְשָׁא בְּרִיךְ הוּא
(בְּרִיךְ הוּא)
לְעֵלָּא מִן כָּל
בִּרְכָתָא וְשִׁירָתָא תֻּשְׁבְּחָתָא וְנֶחֱמָתָא,
דַּאֲמִירָן בְּעָלְמָא. וְאִמְרוּ: אָמֵן
(אָמֵן).
יְהֵא שְׁלָמָא רַבָּא מִן שְׁמַיָּא,
וְחַיִּים עָלֵינוּ וְעַל כָּל יִשְׂרָאֵל.
וְאִמְרוּ: אָמֵן
עוֹשֶׂה שָׁלוֹם בִּמְרוֹמָיו, הוּא יַעֲשֶׂה שָׁלוֹם עָלֵינוּ,
וְעַל כָּל יִשְׂרָאֵל. וְאִמְרוּ: אָמֵן.

May His great Name grow exalted and sanctified

CONGREGATION RESPONDS: Amen

In the world that He created as He willed. May He give reign to His kingship

In your lifetimes and in your days and in the lifetimes of the family of Israel

Swiftly and soon. Now respond: Amen.

CONGREGATION RESPONDS: Amen.

May His great Name be blessed forever and ever; blessed, praised, glorified,

exalted, extolled, upraised, and lauded be the Name of the Holy One,

Blessed is He,

MOURNER'S KADDISH—*all join in*

Yitgadal v'yitkadash sh'mayh rabah.

CONGREGATION RESPONDS: Amen.

B'ol'mo di v'ro chir-utayh.

V'yamlich malchutayh,

B'cha-yaychon uvyomaychon

Uvcha-yay d'chol bayt Yisro-ayl,

Ba-agolo u-vizman koriv.

V'imru: Amen.

CONGREGATION RESPONDS: Amen.

Y'hay sh'mayh rabo m'vorach l'olam ul-ol'may ol'ma-yah.

Yitborach v'yishtabach v'yitpo-ar

V'yitromam v'yitnasay

V'yit-hador v'yit-ale v'yit-halal

Sh-mayh d'kudsho b'rich hu

CONGREGATION RESPONDS: B'rich hu.

L'aylah min kol

Birchata v'shirata tushb'chata v'nechemata,

Da-amiran b'al'ma v'imru: Amen.

CONGREGATION RESPONDS: Amen.

Y'hay sh'lama raba min sh'maya

V'cha-yim olaynu v-al kol Yisra-ayl

V'imru amen.

Oseh shalom bimromav hu ya'aseh shalom aleinu

V'al kol Yisrael v'imru amen.

CONGREGATION RESPONDS: Blessed is He.

Beyond any blessing and song, praise and consolation

that are uttered in the world.

Now respond: Amen.

CONGREGATION RESPONDS: Amen.

May there be abundant peace from heaven, and life, upon us and upon all Israel.

and let us say amen. May He who makes peace in the heavens

make peace upon us and all of Israel,

and let us say, amen.

HATIKVA —all join in

כָּל עוֹד בַּלֵּבָב פְּנִימָה.
נֶפֶשׁ יְהוּדִי הוֹמִיָּה.
וּלְפַאֲתֵי מִזְרָח קָדִימָה.
עַיִן לְצִיּוֹן צוֹפִיָּה:
עוֹד לֹא אָבְדָה תִקְוָתֵנוּ.
הַתִּקְוָה בַּת שְׁנוֹת אַלְפַּיִם.
לִהְיוֹת עַם חָפְשִׁי בְּאַרְצֵנוּ.
אֶרֶץ צִיּוֹן וִירוּשָׁלַיִם:

Kol ode balevov pinema
Nefesh Yehudi homiya
Ulfatay mizrach kadima
Ayin liTzion tzofia
Ode lo avda tikvateynu
Hatikva bat shnot alpayim
Lihyot am chafshi bi-artzaynu
Bi eretz Tzion Yerushalayim

HATIKVA—THE HOPE
As long as in its innermost heart,
The Jewish soul yearns
And toward the eastern corner,
To Zion, his eyes look out
Then our hope is not yet lost
Our hope of two thousand years
To be a free people in our land
The land of Zion and Jerusalem

אבגדההו

חטיכךל

מנסעפ

קרשת